ROYAL REBECCA

igloo

Royal Rebecca was the apple of her parents' eyes. Ever since she was tiny, they had done everything for her.

"You're my little princess," her father often declared, and almost everyone said he treated her like royalty. Other people thought she was just a teensy bit spoilt.

It only took a wave of her royal hand or a nod of her regal head and Rebecca had almost anything she wanted. When she learnt to speak, her nods and waves turned into bossy words.

"Brush my hair! Where are my soldiers?" she snapped at her long-suffering parents.

"Sometimes I think she has ideas above her station, muttered her mother. "We're not servants, after all."

Royal Rebecca liked nothing better than dressing up in her royal robes. She tried to forget that her dad was a humble janitor responsible for the town toilets. She clipped dazzling diamonds to her ears and hung a shiny gold necklace around her neck. She topped it all off with a sparkling tiara.

She imagined she could hear a crowd calling, "We want Rebecca! Long live Royal Rebecca!" She bowed her head slightly, smiled and waved to her people.

Strangely, her most precious possession was an old key her father had given her. It wasn't shiny or jewel-encrusted, but she wore it on an old chain under her sweater. "One day," he said, "it might get you out of a tight spot."

Rebecca behaved in the same regal way wherever she went. She had almost started to believe she really was a princess, and her snooty behaviour sometimes got her into trouble.

One day at school, her teacher Miss Fishlips asked Rebecca to collect the children's books. Rebecca stepped forward reluctantly as the other children laughed.

"Ooh, Miss, Rebecca's too royal to help out!" And then they noticed her shoes. Detective Dave whipped out his magnifying glass and noticed that they were scuffed. . . and Rebecca had often boasted that her servants shined her shoes so brightly she could see her face in them!

 Oh, the shame!

As the class laughed and jeered Miss Fishlips took pity on Rebecca.

"Look who's coming to open the new school library," she said, holding up a picture of a familiar face, topped off with the biggest crown Rebecca had ever seen.

Rebecca's face split into a regal grin.

The Queen! She sighed with pleasure. "Don't you think she looks like me?" she asked Miss Fishlips.
"I think we share the same noble brow, and good taste in jewels."

Later in the staff room, the teachers were discussing the royal visit.

"This is a very important day for Dunlearnin School," declared Mr Cram, the headteacher.

"We must choose the right sort of person to present Her Majesty with flowers. Someone polite, someone gracious, someone almost regal . . ."

Miss Fishlips smiled. "I know just the person," she said.

The great day dawned and Rebecca had prepared well for the royal visit. At last, she had a chance to practise her royal wave in front of a real crowd.

She dressed carefully. "Pass me my jewels, Mama," she said to her mother when she got up.

"Have you shined my shoes, Papa?" she asked her father.

Her parents sighed. They were fed up with Rebecca's royal behaviour.

The Queen's limousine drew upoutside school. The pupils cheered and Rebecca stepped forward to present the bouquet to Her Majesty. She curtsied perfectly and kissed the royal ring. It was the proudest day of her life!

The Queen waved graciously, and then leant forward and whispered in Rebecca's ear.

"My dear, you look like a girl I can trust. Might I ask you the way to the, ahem, throne room?" Rebecca swelled with pride – the Queen was asking her for advice! Then she looked puzzled.

"Begging Your Majesty's pardon, but we don't have a throne, although there are plenty of seats inside."

The Queen turned slightly pink and seemed to cross her legs. "No, no, I think you misunderstand me. I need to powder my nose."

Rebecca still looked blank.

"I need," hissed the Queen, urgently, "the loo!"

Her Majesty seemed very pleased with the gleaming new rest rooms, but disaster struck when she came to leave. The door simply would not budge! She gave it a sharp kick with the royal shoe, and a nervous nudge with the imperial elbow, but it would not open.

"Rebecca!" she called. "Help!"

What a right royal rumpus!

Fireman Blays arrived, clutching his axe.

"Oh dear!" he cried, "What can the matter be?"

"It's the Queen," squeaked Rebecca. "She's stuck in the lavatory."

"Stay calm, Your Majesty! We'll soon have you out."

"Thank you, Fireman Blays. Please as quick as you can. We have to be home at teatime to feed the dogs."

Fireman Blays could not break down the door for fear of covering the Queen in splinters.

Suddenly, Rebecca remembered her key! Before you could say, "God Save the Queen", she had slipped under the door, into the royal cubicle and freed the Queen!

Royal Rebecca had saved the day! Her dad's old key that she always wore was actually the master key to all the toilets in the town.

Before she returned to her castle, the Queen waved what looked suspiciously like a toilet brush.

"We appoint Royal Rebecca the Princess of the Powder Rooms."

'Well done, my little princess," said dad, when she told him about her day.

Rebecca gave her dad a big hug. "It was all thanks to you, Dad. Your old key freed the Queen. She called you the knight of the shining armoire".

also available...

Rude Roger   Dirty Dermot   Pickin' Peter   Space Alien Spike   Silly Sydney   Nude Nigel

Shy Sophie   Cute Candy   Royal Rebecca   Grown-up Gabby   Terrible Twins   Show-off Sharon